a pocketf[ul of]

RHYME

Imagination for a new generation

2006 Poetry Competition for 7-11 year-olds

YoungWriters

Verses From Kent
Edited by Carrie Ghazanfer

 Young**Writers**

First published in Great Britain in 2006 by:
Young Writers
Remus House
Coltsfoot Drive
Peterborough
PE2 9JX
Telephone: 01733 890066
Website: www.youngwriters.co.uk

SB ISBN 1 84602 630 X

Foreword

Young Writers was established in 1991 and has been passionately devoted to the promotion of reading and writing in children and young adults ever since. The quest continues today. Young Writers remains as committed to the nurturing of poetic and literary talent as ever.

This year's Young Writers competition has proven as vibrant and dynamic as ever and we are delighted to present a showcase of the best poetry from across the UK and in some cases overseas. Each poem has been selected from a wealth of *A Pocketful Of Rhyme* entries before ultimately being published in this, our fourteenth primary school poetry series.

Once again, we have been supremely impressed by the overall quality of the entries we have received. The imagination, energy and creativity which has gone into each young writer's entry made choosing the poems a challenging and often difficult but ultimately hugely rewarding task - the general high standard of the work submitted ensured this opportunity to bring their poetry to a larger appreciative audience.

We sincerely hope you are pleased with this final collection and that you will enjoy *A Pocketful Of Rhyme Verses From Kent* for many years to come.

Contents

Bobbing Village School, Sittingbourne

Bredgar CE Primary School, Sittingbourne

Alisha Marsh (10)	38
Luke Seymour (10)	39
Molly O'Neill (10)	40
James Dicey (11)	41
James Lewis (11)	42
Beth Silsbey (9)	43
Anna Mackenzie (11)	44
Holly Coyle (10)	45
Chloe Shaw (10)	46
Harry Constable (10)	47
Sam Henley (11)	48
Edward Henley (10)	49
George Kelly (10)	50
Madeleine Wood (9)	51
Bruce Ford (11)	52

Brenzett CEP School, Brenzett

Jonathan Burgoyne (11)	53

Brookland CE Primary School, Romney Marsh

Jennifer Holmes (10)	54
Emma Louise Maidment (10)	55
Emaley Chantry (11)	56
Sophie Ovenden (10)	57
Amber Blake (9)	58
Laura White (10)	59
Scott Chambers (10)	60
Madeleine Ubee (11)	61

IDE Hill CE Primary School, Sevenoaks

Rhys Jenkins (11)	62
Emili Hone (10)	63
Ella Cocker (10)	64
Liam Cook (11)	65
Dominic Byne (11)	66
Nathan McKerlie (9)	67
Megan Critchlow (10)	68
William Denbigh (10)	69
Felicity Pearson (10)	70

Gemma Symons (10)   71
Sophie Price (11)   72
Tom Kemsley (11)   73
Michael Mills (11)   74

Ightham Primary School, Sevenoaks
Kimberley Wynter (10)   75
Courtney Whitehead (9)   76
Beatrice Harley (8)   77
Callie Birch (10)   78
Olivia Cox (9)   79
Alice Watson (9)   80
Toby Dagnall (9)   81
Liane Smith (11)   82
Claudia Cousins (9)   83
Millie Smith (8)   84

Joy Lane Junior School, Sittingbourne
Louise Clelford (8)   86

Lunsford Primary School, Aylesford
Emma Hance (11)   87
Jack Doyle (11)   88
David Brooks (10)   89
Daniel Lee Banfield (11)   90
Danielle Staples (11)   91
Ryan Banfield (11)   92
Joe Marks (11)   93
Angharad Morgan (10)   94
Emily Farrell (11)   95
Adam Smith (10)   96
Jennifer Glover (11)   97
Gregg Harfleet (10)   98
George Hazelden (11)   99
Claire Martin (10)   100
Jordan Summers (11)   101
Reece Wright (11)   102
Connor Watson (10)   103
Amber Aspinall (11)   104
Katy Millgate (11)   105
Kieron Lee (11)   106

Hannah Friel (11) 107
Leanne Ring (11) 108
Amy Hadley (11) 109
Shannon George (10) 110
Luke Body (11) 111
Nicole Johnston (11) 112
Sophie Rideout (11) 113
Rachel Jones (11) 114

Pembury Primary School, Tunbridge Wells

Connor Fitzgerald (10) 115
Toby White (11) 116
Hannah Lancaster (10) 117
Kathryn Lawson-Wood (11) 118
Bethany Lambert (11) 119
Bethany Pike (11) 120
Catherine Goldsmith (11) 121

Sibertswold CE Primary School, Dover

Lucy Gilchrist (10) 122
Charlotte Powell (10) 123
Emily Coupe (11) 124
Becky Brown (9) 125
Luke Firth-Coppock (10) 126
Annabel Reville (10) 127
Shannah Hall (10) 128
Tom Harman (10) 129
Claire Penny (9) 130
Ruby Russell (10) 131
Abigail McLean (10) 132
Laura Palmer (10) 133
Daniel Westbrook (9) 134
Amy Hill (9) 135
Hannah Coupe (9) 136
Laura Winter (9) 137
Sarah Penny (10) 138
Thomas Duncan (8) 139
Charles Harman (9) 140
Jonathan Allen (9) 141
Wil Green (9) 142
Jordan Witts (9) 143

Daisy Hobbs (9)   144
Jacob Roberts (9)   145
Alexander Byrne (9)   146
Harry Miller (9)   147
Jessica Doble (10)   148
Laura Castledine (9)   149
Hannah Butcher (9)   150
Courtney Forrest (8)   151
Stuart Lindsay (9)   152
Jack Miller (8)   153
Remy Beasley (9)   154

St Augustine of Canterbury Catholic Primary School, Gillingham
Connor Stickings (11)   155
Georgie Brace (11)   156
Katherine Parry (11)   157
Megan Gough (10)   158
Lauren Catherine Chamberlain (10)   159
Daniel Johnston (11)   160
Sam James Crockford (10)   161
Samuel Richardson (9)   162
Jacob Hart-Lane (10)   163
Emily Louisa Fallon (9)   164
Alice Sivyer (10)   165
Shane Cox (10)   166

St Michael's CE Junior School, Maidstone
Hannah Wadey (8)   167

St Peter's Catholic Primary School, Sittingbourne
Laura Sage (11)   168
Anthony Burbury (10)   169
Matthew Jones (11)   170
Matthew Burbury (10)   171
Lachlan Hutton (11)   172
Tom Farren (11)   173
Ben Avery (10)   174
Nicola Rodgers (10)   175
David Robertson (10)   176
David Williams (10)   177
Abimbola Ogunyemi (9)   178

Poppi-Anna Conway (10)	179
Ellie Haddock (9)	180
Grace Butcher (10)	181
Poppy Byrne (10)	182
Lauren Etherington (10)	183
Christopher Harimat (9)	184
Heather Barton (10)	185
Zoe Thomas (10)	186
Layla-Autumn Harris (10)	187
Brieanna Way (10)	188
Tom Sewell (10)	189
Eleanor Page (10)	190
Deborah Shangobiyi (10)	191

West Malling Primary School, West Malling

Joe Chapman (10)	192
Megan Locke (10)	193
Harry Stansfield (10)	194
Amy Thompson (11)	195
Zoey Nettleingham (10)	196
Tom Steer (11)	197
Chloe Cooke (11)	198

The Poems

Lollipop

A curly colourful twister,
Wrapped in a see-through wrapper,
Get a grip, tear off the wrapper
And where has the lollipop gone?

Natalie Towers (9)
Bobbing Village School, Sittingbourne

My Family

My dad is a worker,
He works all day, non-stop,
He plays on games sometimes,
My dad is quite funny,
He is the best,
I love him more than life.

I love my mum, more than life,
My mum likes plants,
She helps me with my homework,
She is the best mum in the world,
My mum likes gardening programmes.

I love my sister, more than life,
She likes playing games with me,
She is quite moany,
She has a talent for being good.

Benjamin David (10)
Bobbing Village School, Sittingbourne

This Poem

My intelligence keeps on going
And I'm trying to write a poem,
I need some ideas,
I need some ideas,
To write this poem,
My intelligence keeps on going
And I have to write
This poem.

Abbey Leadbetter (10)
Bobbing Village School, Sittingbourne

The End Of The World

I opened my curtains,
I stopped, I listened,
I stared, frightened and shocked,
What a scene there was.

People were running around,
This way, that way,
Faces drained of colour,
Eyes wide and blank.

Flames licked the sky,
Buildings began to crumble,
People's livelihoods disappeared,
Left in piles of rubble.

Reece Burrows (11)
Bobbing Village School, Sittingbourne

My Mum

My mum is the best,
She looks after me,
She cooks for me,
She is there for me.

Roses are red,
Violets are blue,
Do you love me?
Because I love you.

Michael Goatham (10)
Bobbing Village School, Sittingbourne

The Bully From The Past Year

The past year,
I've had fear,
From this bully.

She's mean,
She's cruel,
She likes to rule.

I'm sad,
She's bad,
My parents are mad.

She's in my maths group,
She's got two other bullies
For her troop.

Jodie East (10)
Bobbing Village School, Sittingbourne

Shadows

I've watched life go by,
Sitting on a bench, time will fly,
I looked by on the road,
I want to go and live in hell,
I'm old, shadows pass me all the time.

I'm writhing in pain, I have no legs,
My arms are wasted and not amputated yet,
Everything passes me, I'm going to die,
Lord can't you end this?
My life swivelling, these shadows are not bliss.

Guy Wakefield (11)
Bobbing Village School, Sittingbourne

Christmas

I am a festival,
Which is very important,
I am a festival,
That cheers people up,
I turn frowns upside down
And make sure they are celebrating.

Snow drops in this festival,
Followed by ice hung on treetops,
Holly is picked and hung in the house,
Turkey roasting all day long,
Greeting presents and cards,
Cheer children up, makes them smile,
I am celebrated by Christians,
What am I?

Answer: Christmas Day.

Andy Li (10)
Bobbing Village School, Sittingbourne

Late

I go to school,
Book screamed 'Give in homework,'
'Can't!' I said, 'Late!'

Have lunch,
Lunch box said 'Eat now,'
'Can't!' I said, 'Late!'

PE today,
PE kit yelled 'Put me on!'
'Can't!' I said, 'Late!'

Go to bed,
Pillow calls me 'Come to bed,'
'Night everyone!'

Georgie Louise Elder (10)
Bobbing Village School, Sittingbourne

Valentine's Day

Love, hugs and kisses,
Valentine's wishes,
Cards, chocolates and love hearts,
Dancing with your partners and
Eating jam tarts.

Now the day is over,
All the love has gone,
But then your boyfriend comes
And sings you a song.

Paige Evans (11)
Bobbing Village School, Sittingbourne

Why Me?

Why am I so lonely?
Sitting here, looking at my phone,
Why am I so alone?

At school, everyone moves away,
Not noticing me at all,
Why am I so alone?

Why me?

No one there for me at all,
No one anymore,
Why am I so alone?

No one to talk to,
I keep wondering why,
Why am I so alone?

Why me?

Roxxanna Lang (10)
Bobbing Village School, Sittingbourne

My Pet Is . . .

My pet has a tail,
My pet has 4 legs,
My pet doesn't fly,
My pet is scaly,
My pet is one,
You won't forget,
It is a green,
Horribly mean,
Strictly clean,
Naughty, lean,
Killing machine.

Eliot Budgen & Liam Gardner (9)
Bobbing Village School, Sittingbourne

Stars

Always there, but not always seen,
Waiting for the night,
To twinkle so bright,
There's the moon,
They will be here soon,
Look at them, so bright,
Up at the sky at night,
Slowly going,
Day is coming.

Hannah Crawford (9)
Bobbing Village School, Sittingbourne

Why Should I Be Bullied?

At school there's a bully called Frank,
He always gives me a spank,
He always picks on me
And the teachers don't do anything,
Except watch and see,
Why should I be bullied?

In my class, there's a girl who makes fun of me,
She says my hair is rougher than the sea,
She says my clothes are old
And they should be sold,
Why should I be bullied?

I can't put up with this,
I'm going to make a stand,
Why should everywhere I go be bully-land?
I'm not going to be bullied anymore,
I'm not going to come home very sore,
Why should I be bullied?

I stood up to the bullies, they fight me no more,
I am no longer sore,
No one bullies me
And I've got lots of friends to see.

Kelsey Crehan (11)
Bobbing Village School, Sittingbourne

Dreams!

They're all locked inside,
They are in a constant hide.

Dreams are inside
And they have no key,
No key from your heart to your head.

They are all locked inside,
All trapped with no voice,
No say in what they do!

Come out!
Come out!
Come walk about!

We can't!
We can't!
We're trapped inside!
Only you can set us free!

Eleanor Grimshaw (10)
Bobbing Village School, Sittingbourne

Referees!

Refs are bad,
They think they're cool,
They think they rule the game,
But they don't at all.

All those cards, are we meant to be scared?
All those rules are getting boring.

Refs are bad,
Refs are bad,
If you agree shout, 'Get it right!'

Andrew McGrath (10)
Bobbing Village School, Sittingbourne

Where Is The Love?

Where is the love in the world?
It suddenly disappeared,
All the graffiti on the walls,
Let's get it all cleared up!
Because there are people with guns,
They should be locked up,
There's people free and running away,
Now ask yourself a question,
Where is the love?

Jack Newcombe (9)
Bobbing Village School, Sittingbourne

Dolphin

Dolphin, dolphin,
You swim in the sea,
Dolphin, dolphin,
You could never hurt me,
Dolphin, dolphin,
You like the water,
Dolphin, dolphin,
I've never fought you,
Dolphin, dolphin,
You're my best friend,
Dolphin, dolphin,
It will never end.

Daniel Ballard   (10)
Bobbing Village School, Sittingbourne

Dawn Of War

Orbs are viscous killers,
Who fight to their deaths,
They will rush in with an axe.

Space Martians are the emperor's
Chosen troops
Who will always defend him.

Chaos Martians are evil,
Soldiers that fight too,
Take over the world.

Elders are fighters of peace
And believe strongly in a very peaceful faith.

Imperial guards are ordered to
Back space Martians and they are human.

Callum Daniel Austin (9)
Bobbing Village School, Sittingbourne

Spaghetti

It slithers down my throat like a skinny snake,
The flavour's hot and saucy, making me dribble,
Just make a big plate of it so I can eat,
Yum, yum, yum! Goes right into my tum, lots go in,
Spaghetti, you're number 1 on my list!

Beth Keenan (9)
Bobbing Village School, Sittingbourne

How Football Has Lived

Football was made by an Englishman,
Who was always thinking of new games,
So one day he was cooking in his frying pan
And thought of a good game with quite a cool name.

Football, football, it's the best,
When you play, you're on a quest,
Football, football, it's the best!

He got a ball and made a goal,
Then he built a stadium,
Wembley's the name, just one big hole,
So he priced up the things in one big sum.

Football, football, it's the best,
When you play, you'll run with your vest,
Football, football, it's the best!

So as time went on, stuff was advanced,
Everything was improved,
You needed to look at Wembley, just one glance,
Then all the teams got better so many players moved.

Football, football, it's the best,
Now when you play, it's the best,
Football, football, it's the best!

Beau Taylor (10)
Bobbing Village School, Sittingbourne

The Rap That I Told About Hate

I was on the streets one day,
My mother kicked me out,
Since I've been there,
I've been hanging about.

All my friends are still in their houses,
Everybody hates me,
I just want somebody to love me,
I want to be somebody.

A few weeks later,
The police found me,
I was adopted,
To a family.

I am so happy,
Thank you world for
Caring about me!

Folu Irinoye (9)
Bobbing Village School, Sittingbourne

The Glorious Knight

He has a very sharp sword,
He kills people who commit fraud,
He has spiky hair,
The king doesn't care.

What shall he do when he's in trouble?
Call his horse, they kill on the double,
His horse is brown,
He kills the king and nicks his crown.

People are dancing,
He starts prancing,
He gets a wife,
She tries killing him with a knife.

George Myers (10)
Bobbing Village School, Sittingbourne

The Sea Is . . .

A golden coin is reflecting,
On the glazed blue sea.

The sea is like blue jelly
Wibbling and wobbling,
Like the blue waves smashing.

And that's that!

Phoebe Humphrey (9)
Bobbing Village School, Sittingbourne

Touch The Sky

The sun, the sun,
Glistening so bright.

The moon so dull,
The stars so high.

You know I wanna touch the sky.

Animals are roaming,
Athletes are running
Fish are swimming.

You know I wanna touch the sky.

Swordfish are fighting,
Whales are humming,
Dolphins are calling.

You know I wanna touch the sky.

Hairdressers are cutting,
Cooks are cooking,
Singers are singing.

You know I wanna touch the sky.

Amy Honey (10)
Bobbing Village School, Sittingbourne

My Friend!

My friend has brown plaited hair and brown eyes,
She has a baby hamster at home called Snowy,
She is sometimes silent and sometimes loud . . .
But she will always be my best friend
Whatever happens!

And that is what makes me warm inside!

Sarah Reynolds (10)
Bobbing Village School, Sittingbourne

My Friend

He has spiky hair that is black,
He's good at games like bumper cars,
He aims at me all the time and he pin balls
Me with my other mate Jack,
When he's coming towards me
I bumper car him out the way,
But it never works because of
Casey who likes to be called Fish.

Do you know who the mystery mate is?
George!

Bill John Spooner (9)
Bobbing Village School, Sittingbourne

How I Miss You Grandad

Grandad, how surprised were you when you found out?
I was surprised, very surprised.

How scared were you when you found out?
I was very scared, maybe you were too!

How much did you know about the disease?
I didn't know a lot, did you?

The anger I felt was so strong, like a fire,
That they couldn't help you!

The love I feel will go on for eternity,
I hope yours will too!

At the funeral, I felt every emotion you can,
I love you Grandad.

Thank you for saying me and my brother
Were your holy lights.
Thank you.

Charlotte Smith (9)
Bobbing Village School, Sittingbourne

Fast Bikes, Slow Bike

Motorbikes are fast,
Motorbikes carry 1 or 2 people,
That is all,
Motorbikes go fast,
There are so many types,
You just lose control,
They are fast, they are slow,
They just make you lose control,
Bikes are like cars,
They have an engine,
Motorbikes can be fast or slow,
They just make you lose control!

Jordan Clifford (9)
Bobbing Village School, Sittingbourne

My Killer Animal

He is always in films,
He does excellent tricks in the water,
He lives in the big ocean,
He is the friend for me,
He is the killing machine.
A killer whale!

Casey Fuller (10)
Bobbing Village School, Sittingbourne

Grumpy Old Men

There was once an old man from Spain,
Who was in a lot of pain,
So he packed his bag and said 'Goodbye'
And we never saw him again.

There was an old man from York,
Who had a knife and fork,
He was in a mood, so he didn't eat his food,
Poor old man from York.

Kyle Maryott (10)
Bobbing Village School, Sittingbourne

My Hamster

My hamster is white,
Like snow,
His name is Snowy,
He has pink ears and feet,
With bobbly feet,
He's my best friend,
Just like Sarah,
She has blonde hair and
Blue eyes
And that is that!

Naomi Brockett (10)
Bobbing Village School, Sittingbourne

My Nan

Nan when you went, my heart was broken,
I felt like a part was missing.

Nan why did you go?
Why did you go?

I miss you, my life is not the same,
No cuddles, no songs, no bus trips.

Nan why did you go?
Why did you go?

Now you're in Heaven, I hope you watch
Down on me, Nanny I love you!

Charlotte Wilson (10)
Bobbing Village School, Sittingbourne

My Name

Read this poem and see what you can find out about me!

K is for a kite drifting in the sky,
A is for the start of the alphabet,
T is for when you're alone and you feel tiny,
I is for myself in the first tense,
E is for the end of my story about myself.

What have you found out about me?

Katie Ginn   (10)
Bobbing Village School, Sittingbourne

Sadness

Sadness is when your family argue,
Sadness is when you friends betray you,
Sadness is when you feel ill,
Sadness is when someone's died,
Sadness is when your heart breaks,
Sadness is when you are bullied,
But most of all, sadness is when no one is smiling,
Because peace begins with a smile.

Melissa Luker (11)
Bobbing Village School, Sittingbourne

Grey Days

I hate grey days,
They are really annoying,
No one is enjoying them,
Stuck indoors, doing nothing,
Besides playing dress-up and cooking muffins,
I suppose they are not all that bad,
There is no point in being sad,
You can always find something to do,
Even if I watch my sister put on a shoe,
Well at least it will be sunny soon.

Samual Smith (11)
Bobbing Village School, Sittingbourne

Symone

S he is sent down from Heaven,
Y ou are my best friend,
M oaning she does not do,
O utgoing and active,
N ever judges people,
E veryone's her friend.

God bless you!

Samantha Mann (11)
Bobbing Village School, Sittingbourne

Animals

Hipperty hop,
Hipperty hop,
A frog jumps down
And jumped on the log.

Galloping horse,
Galloping horse,
Jumped over the fence
And around the course.

Waddly duck,
Waddly duck,
Swam in the sparkling river,
The laughing duck got stuck.

Bouncy rabbit,
Bouncy rabbit,
Goes down his tunnelled home,
The rabbit saw it and decided to grab it.

Miaowing cat,
Miaowing cat,
Used his claws to scratch,
The cat had a special black and white bat.

Woofing dog,
Woofing dog,
The dog woofed for its lovely meat,
Sloppy food.

Running cheetahs,
Running cheetahs,
Running all around,
The cheetahs were even faster than the beaters.

Alisha Marsh (10)
Bredgar CE Primary School, Sittingbourne

Bredgar School

Bredgar School is sometimes fun,
In lunch you get a currant bun.

The only thing I don't like,
Is the work, like when we do it
My mate acts like a burk!

I get back home and
My little sister's being a pain,
I go out to play and
I come home saying,
'It's lame!'

B rilliant,
R oaring,
E lephantastic,
D oogley,
A great school
R eally.

I go to sleep and my baby brother is screaming
I say 'Shut up' and he starts weeping.

Then I go to sleep thinking of the boring day tomorrow.

Luke Seymour (10)
Bredgar CE Primary School, Sittingbourne

Zoo Animals

A ll animals are cute,
N ewts slither like little water snakes,
I guanas are creepy like little dinosaurs,
M ammoths are big and fluffy,
A ntelopes are big and scary,
L ions are like newborn baby kittens,
S nakes slither on the cold kitchen floor.

A pes are weird,
R ats are small and annoying,
E lephants are big and loud.

G iraffes have long necks like lamp posts,
R abbits hop and stop,
E lephants are friendly but look scary,
A nacondas are big, mean and scary,
T ortoises are too slow to win a race.

Molly O'Neill (10)
Bredgar CE Primary School, Sittingbourne

The Big Match

The crowd is silent and expectant as he
Delivers the ball up the pitch,
He's tackled by Ronaldinho,
He's tackled him back and gets the ball back,
He dribbles it up the pitch and round Belleti.

He's in the box,
He shoots,
The keeper misses the ball,
He scores!
The whistle blows,
They've won,
He wakes up from his daydream,
He puts on his number 11 shirt and walks
Out onto the pitch . . .

James Dicey (11)
Bredgar CE Primary School, Sittingbourne

In The Playground

The girls are skipping,
Boys daydreaming,
The teachers are toads,
The ball's in the road,
The teachers are in the class,
They are looking out of the glass,
The ugly school bully,
Is beating up Woolly,
Tom is skipping,
The teachers are whipping,
That silly boy called Sam,
Is always eating ham,
The computers are bleeping,
That boy called Bruce is weeping,
Teacher's on the phone,
Now it's time for home.

James Lewis (11)
Bredgar CE Primary School, Sittingbourne

My Cat Fudge!

M y favourite black and white cat,
Y ou can tell when she's wet,
    as she looks like a drowned rat!

C arefully licking her silky black fur,
A ngry when she finds she's going to the vet!
T ail swishing as birds swoop down.

F unny when she smells another cat on her territory!
U nique in every single way,
D evil when she's on the mat, as she rips it apart,
G enerous and beautiful is my black and white cat,
E ver so cute as she dreams on and on.

Beth Silsbey (9)
Bredgar CE Primary School, Sittingbourne

Happiness

Happiness is like going for a long, relaxing walk along
damp golden sand in the moonlight.
Happiness is like when you go swimming in the crystal,
clear blue, foamy sea, and feeling the grainy brown
sand beneath your feet.

Happiness is like riding a bike, freewheeling down
a massive hill.
Happiness is when you see the first yellow daffodil,
staring up into the springtime sun.

Happiness is like when brightly coloured flowers,
nod at you happily in the warm summer's breeze.
Happiness is like when you look out of a window
and see a clear blue, cloudless sky.

Happiness is like white, frozen, crunchy snow
when it has fallen on Christmas Day.
Happiness is waking up to lots of lovely presents
on your birthday that you have been waiting for,
for such a long time.

Anna Mackenzie (11)
Bredgar CE Primary School, Sittingbourne

Giraffes

G iraffes are cute,
 I would enjoy playing with a giraffe,
R olling about in all the leaves
A nd to remember that time would be good too.
F ooling about and . . .
F ollowing their mum's tails,
E nding their lives with happiness and . . .
S eeing everyone with their big eyes.

Holly Coyle (10)
Bredgar CE Primary School, Sittingbourne

Lions And Cubs

L ions are lazy,
I n the hot sun,
O ver the savannah,
N ew fresh water, that they lap up carefully over the horizon,
S leepy and snoozy he drifts off into a sleep.

A ngry lions bite each other's tail,
N aughty lion cubs, playing tricks,
D ad has a mane bushy and big.

C ubs are playful,
U nsure about leaving the den,
B eing careful not to scare their prey away,
S eeing their mother who is calling them to bed.

Chloe Shaw (10)
Bredgar CE Primary School, Sittingbourne

Wigs

Gregory Grigs, Gregory Grigs,
Has twenty-seven different wigs,
He wore them up, he wore them down,
To please the people of the town,
But Gregory Grigs, Gregory Grigs,
Could not find his favourite wigs,
Gregory Grigs, Gregory Grigs,
Owner of twenty-seven different wigs,
Looked up high, looked down low
And found it inside the Teletubbie *Po*.

Harry Constable (10)
Bredgar CE Primary School, Sittingbourne

Guess Who?

Lives in Spain,
Wife is vain,
England's skipper,
Penalty kicker,
Right wing,
Fast thing,
Long hair,
Is fair,
Real star,
Fancy car,
Number seven,
Lives in Heaven,
Loves Posh,
Married to dosh,
Good in the air
And plays with flare,
Free kick taker,
Goal maker,
England star,
Will go far,
He's better than you,
Now guess who?

A: David Beckham.

Sam Henley (11)
Bredgar CE Primary School, Sittingbourne

My Monster

He's very tall,
He slithers and crawls,
That's my monster,
Better than them all.

Crunch! Crunch!
Munch! Munch!
That's the way my
Monster gobbles his lunch.

He's the very best
And wears a grubby vest,
I like him very much,
Even though he's Dutch.

Crunch! Crunch!
Munch! Munch!
That's the way my
Monster gobbles his lunch.

He sits on the couch like a slob,
Because he doesn't have a good job,
He wants to be mega cool,
But he acts like a stupid fool.

Crunch! Crunch!
Munch! Munch!
That's the way my
Monster eats his lunch.

He likes to splash in puddles,
While getting into muddles,
He will be dead tomorrow,
My eyes are full of sorrow.

Edward Henley (10)
Bredgar CE Primary School, Sittingbourne

Sports

S wimming is wet, like a goldfish in a tank,
P ool is tactical, like trying to climb Mount Everest,
O lympics is challenging, like walking a tightrope,
R ugby is tough, like lifting a boulder,
T ennis is fast, like Speedy Gonzalez,
S occer is priceless, like a diamond in a tomb.

George Kelly (10)
Bredgar CE Primary School, Sittingbourne

Flamingos

F lamingos are pink,
L ike a pink rose,
A load of pink rows,
M any flamingos,
I n a big pen,
N ine hundred pink feathers,
G reen wetlands where they live,
O nly flamingos can stand on one leg,
S ee them in the zoo and you'll love them too!

Madeleine Wood (9)
Bredgar CE Primary School, Sittingbourne

Snow

Snow is falling,
Winter is calling,
There it lays,
Waiting for the next day.

It's six o'clock,
The ground is like an immense sheep flock,
Just like silk,
It's the colour of fresh milk.

People are bolting outside,
Quick! Dive deep and hide,
Grab a pearl-white snowball,
If you hit they will fall.

Bruce Ford (11)
Bredgar CE Primary School, Sittingbourne

Skeletons

Skeletons are cool,
Skeletons are fun,
They are really bony
And they're number one.

Why are people scared of them?
They are so extremely cool,
I'd really like one as a friend
And take it to my school.

Skeletons are cool,
Skeletons are fun,
They are really bony
And they're number one.

I've heard they are good dancers,
They like to groovy down,
Although when they start playing footie,
They look like they are a clown.

Skeletons are cool,
Skeletons are fun,
They are really bony
And they're number one.

I really love skeletons,
They're cool, fun and lanky,
They have great bodies,
But they can be rather cranky.

Skeletons are cool,
Skeletons are fun,
They are really bony
And they're number one.

Jonathan Burgoyne (11)
Brenzett CEP School, Brenzett

I Wish I Were An Actress

I wish I were an actress,
With lots of sparkling dresses
And blue, posh high heels,
Posing for the presses.

Later on that evening,
I'd have a beauty mask,
Put on my silky pyjamas
And think about the past.

I'd have won 5 Oscars
And walked down the red carpet,
I'd have a golden Labrador,
As my loyal friendly pet.

Jennifer Holmes (10)
Brookland CE Primary School, Romney Marsh

The Wet Young Lady Of Wales

There was a young lady of Wales,
Who had a boat with 10 sails,
For she started to row,
When the wind started to blow,
That wet young lady of Wales.

Emma Louise Maidment (10)
Brookland CE Primary School, Romney Marsh

The Weather

Some shall have water and rain,
Some shall have sun and air,
Some shall have seas and oceans
And that's the weather.

Some shall have rivers and lakes,
Some shall have thunder and lightning,
Some shall have snow and hail
And that's the weather.

Some shall have twisters and tornadoes,
Some shall have ice and frost,
Some have storms and rumbles
And that's the weather.

Emaley Chantry (11)
Brookland CE Primary School, Romney Marsh

Blue Pekins

Down the bottom of my green garden,
There my Blue Pekins will rest,
Gleaming their silky blue feathers,
Until they're at their best.

All my four Pekins have names,
For instance, little old Mini Maisie,
Who fell in love with Mental Mickey,
Who is really very crazy.

I also have a pale Blue Pekin,
Whose name is Mini May,
Whose best friend is Mini Emma,
Who has only just started to lay.

I love all my chickens equally,
Especially after yesterday,
When suddenly I got four eggs,
Is my cockerel starting to lay?

Sophie Ovenden (10)
Brookland CE Primary School, Romney Marsh

The Dolphin

Underneath the pure blue sea,
Bathes a dolphin in the sand,
I get on his back and he swims with me,
As I stroke him with my hand.

He stops and shivers at a cliff,
Where I get off his back and look around,
I peer around at the top of the cliff
And I can't hear a single sound.

I tell the dolphin not to worry,
As I see something with a striped case,
It read on the metal container *Danger!*
Don't touch, toxic waste!

Amber Blake (9)
Brookland CE Primary School, Romney Marsh

Lonely Puppy

Lonely puppy sitting in the street,
Feeding off rubbish and rotten meat,
Wanders the streets day and night,
Ever so lonely, poor little mite.

Sees owners playing with their dogs,
For comfort he pictures a fire with logs,
Nobody listens to his tiny bark,
As he sits alone in the dark.

Poor old puppy wishes he had some friends,
Wishes he knew how to make amends,
The horrid owner didn't love him anymore,
So he kicked the puppy out the door.

Poor little puppy is all alone,
Wishes he had a proper home,
Wanders the streets day and night,
Ever so lonely, poor little mite.

Laura White (10)
Brookland CE Primary School, Romney Marsh

Incredible Old Trafford

Incredible Old Trafford,
Home to great football players,
Famous, legendary, large,
As noisy as a thousand beating drums,
As huge as one hundred cars stuck in a traffic jam on the M20,
It makes me feel quiet,
Almost invisible,
Incredible Old Trafford,
Makes me think about everyone who's been there.

Scott Chambers (10)
Brookland CE Primary School, Romney Marsh

Rubbish

Rubbish seems to be different things,
Paper, gloves and chicken wings.

Mouldy food and muddy bags,
Broken pots and burnt out fags.

Empty cans and glass thrown down,
Left by drunks out on the town.

Owners of dogs don't clean up their poo,
You step on their mess and it sticks to your shoe.

The homeless in the morning leave their cardboard boxes,
With bits of old food in that attract the foxes.

Teenagers spitting their chewing gum out,
'Leave the streets tidy' I just want to shout.

Walking along as they whisper and mutter,
Leaving their rubbish thrown down in the gutter.

On the beach at the end of the day,
Dirty nappies often lay.

Ripped wrapped and melted lollies,
Wet shorts and broken dollies.

Recycling our rubbish is one thing we must do,
To keep our country looking as good as new.

Madeleine Ubee (11)
Brookland CE Primary School, Romney Marsh

Bowling

I really enjoy bowling,
I think it's really great,
Every time I have a turn,
I seem to get a strike,
Even when it's not my go,
My luck does not run out,
Even the professionals,
I always seem to clout!
My favourite bowling place,
Is Tunbridge Wells Bowlplex,
Sometimes I'm not so lucky,
I barely knock down three,
All the other players,
Seem to do better than me.

Rhys Jenkins (11)
IDE Hill CE Primary School, Sevenoaks

Waterfall

In the mountains,
In the hills,
There's lots of fish,
In the waterfall,
Its rocky surface,
Great to see,
Tomorrow we'll go there,
Just you and me.

Emili Hone (10)
IDE Hill CE Primary School, Sevenoaks

The Pigeon

I went to school one day,
I went to go and play,
There was something on the ground,
Everyone crowded around.

I found out it was a pigeon,
A very talented pigeon,
He had tags around his feet,
He was very nice to meet.

We looked after him very well,
He got scared when we rang the bell,
We gave him lots of water,
We named this pigeon Walter.

Ella Cocker (10)
IDE Hill CE Primary School, Sevenoaks

Racing Pigeon

P layground pigeon,
I ts name is Walter,
G reat fun to have him around!
E ven when he flies away,
O n the wall we'll have a picture of him,
N ever will we forget him!

Liam Cook (11)
IDE Hill CE Primary School, Sevenoaks

Space

I'd love to go to space,
Explore the stars and the moon,
Be an astronaught, meet martians
And eat spaceman food.

I'd love to go to space,
Explore the galaxy so far,
Zap meteors, float around
And eat water on Mars.

I'd love to go to space,
But that will never happen,
I'm poor, I'm silly, I'm rugged,
I'll never go that far.

Dominic Byne (11)
IDE Hill CE Primary School, Sevenoaks

Pigeon In The Playground

One cloudy day,
I was out at play,
I saw a pigeon,
It was grey.

My teacher told us to be careful,
For we were running wild,
But the day was mild.

This is no ordinary pigeon,
This is a racing pigeon,
But his best friend was a robin,
Who ran off sobbing.

Nathan McKerlie (9)
IDE Hill CE Primary School, Sevenoaks

Walter The Pigeon

Walter the pigeon is a friend,
I met him at school one day,
He was very tired and needed a rest,
So he stopped off at our school to rest and play.

Walter tends to bounce around,
Hopping, waddling along the ground,
Chirping, cheeping, wanting more friends,
Never, ever drives me round the bend.

Then one day it started to rain,
Poor Walter the pigeon
Cheeps,
Not again.

Later that day,
Off he went
And says *thank you for the water and food,*
That you lent.

Megan Critchlow (10)
IDE Hill CE Primary School, Sevenoaks

Pigeon In The Playground

One sunny day,
Out at play,
I saw a funny bird,
But never to be heard was the funny bird.

The teacher told us off,
For chasing the little animal,
Is he a reptile or a mammal?
He came from a country with lots of camels.

He had a big head
And his favourite food was bread
And he had a friend who was an eagle,
Who only lived on bagels.

But what is he?
A pigeon.

William Denbigh (10)
IDE Hill CE Primary School, Sevenoaks

Socks

Stripy, spotty,
Going mad.

In smelly wellies,
I smell so bad.

Odd socks,
Rather sad.

Ugly socks,
All from Dad.

Woolly socks,
From the old lad.

My friends all say,
'They look really bad.'

Felicity Pearson (10)
IDE Hill CE Primary School, Sevenoaks

Walter The Pigeon

Walter, Walter,
Pigeon from far,
Came to IDE Hill School.

Walter, Walter,
He loves the fuss,
Everyone came round, it's Walter!

Walter, Walter,
Here to stay
Forever and a day!

Gemma Symons (10)
IDE Hill CE Primary School, Sevenoaks

Spring

Spring is the time when the sun comes out,
It's the time when you can finally get out and about,
You can now play outside
And go to parks and on the rides,
Spring is the time for sun.

In spring, lambs are born,
In spring, farmers pick the corn,
Spring is a time for fun.

Sophie Price (11)
IDE Hill CE Primary School, Sevenoaks

Walter

We saw a pigeon in the sky,
It landed on our playground,
The little pigeon looked so lost
And it landed on my bags
And we named it Walter,
It drank lots of water,
I will be so sad when it flies away.

Tom Kemsley (11)
IDE Hill CE Primary School, Sevenoaks

Grannies

G rannies are old and wrinkly,
R eally annoying when they want to kiss you,
A lways like a good chat,
N ever forget birthdays,
N ever ever really clean their teeth,
I ncapable of remembering our names,
E xtremely kind and generous,
S o actually, that's why we love them!

Michael Mills (11)
IDE Hill CE Primary School, Sevenoaks

What Am I?

I can be lots of different colours,
I am used to dry people,
I am usually warm and really soft,
I am really quite cosy.

I comfort people when they leave the shower,
As he or she might be cold,
You can have small or big ones of me,
So what could I be?

A towel!

Kimberley Wynter (10)
Ightham Primary School, Sevenoaks

When I Think Of My Mum

My mum is precious and important to me,
She makes me feel as happy as can be,
She cheers me up when I am sad,
Her smiles and laughter make me glad,
When I think of my mum,
She works so hard throughout the years,
She gets me over all my fears,
She wipes away my crying tears,
My lovely, pretty mum.

Courtney Whitehead (9)
Ightham Primary School, Sevenoaks

Seasons

S easons are very good fun,
E veryone has excitement
A nd everyone has something special,
S ome have birthdays, some have holidays,
O f course everyone has something,
N one have nothing.

Beatrice Harley (8)
Ightham Primary School, Sevenoaks

The Beach

The sea glimmers all of the day,
All the children come and play,
Lots of people trying to sail,
Follow the sand footprint trail,
To all the people playing with kites,
I think it's time for a water fight,
Go and swim in the sea,
All the waves splashing up at me,
Get an ice cream at the van,
Go and eat it on the sand,
Time to go,
Wave goodbye!

Callie Birch (10)
Ightham Primary School, Sevenoaks

Snow

Snow is so soft,
It is cold in your fingers.

So wet and white,
Comes so little in the year.

It only lasts a couple of minutes,
In the hot sun's beam.

So lovely and peaceful,
Relaxing and dead.

A light white sheen,
So beautiful and pretty.

Olivia Cox (9)
Ightham Primary School, Sevenoaks

When I Think Of My Mum

She's supported me through all these years,
She's helped me overcome my fears,
She always puts a smile upon my face,
She taught me how to tie a lace,
When I think of my mum,
Every day I love her more,
She helps me when my knee is sore,
I love her lots and she's the best,
That could only be my mum.

Alice Watson (9)
Ightham Primary School, Sevenoaks

My Dad Is Mad

My dad is mad,
It can be bad,
But he cheers me up when I'm sad.

He watches birds,
He loves lemon curd
And together we make up funny words.

My dad is mad,
It's sometimes bad,
But he does cheer me up when I'm sad.

He tells silly jokes
And if I'm sipping Coke,
I laugh till I choke,
Because he's really quite a funny bloke.

My dad is mad,
It's not too bad,
Because he always cheers me up when I'm sad.

He looks in the sky,
To see what's flying by,
While sitting in fields of barley and rye.

My dad is mad,
Which occasionally can be bad,
Although he'll definitely cheer me up when I'm sad.

He loves interesting flowers
And we like making towers,
He's my Jedi Knight but he doesn't have supernatural powers . . .

My dad is mad,
It's really not that bad
And do you know, I'm really glad.

I can count on my dad when I'm sad.

Toby Dagnall (9)
Ightham Primary School, Sevenoaks

Seasons

Summer
Summer is the season of goodwill and joy,
People come out with their favourite toys,
Summer is mainly very sunny,
The ice cream man gets lots of money.

Autumn
Autumn is very mild,
The leaves are all piled,
Autumn is very cold,
Children aren't allowed out, that's what they're told.

Winter
Winter is the season when you find presents on the ground
And when people put on a pound!
Winter's when snow's about,
Not many people are about.

Spring
Spring is when the bees come out,
That's when people usually shout,
All the seasons are about,
Love, goodwill and joy.

Liane Smith (11)
Ightham Primary School, Sevenoaks

Evana Who Lives In A Hotel

My name is Evana and I live at the Tipton,
It's a very special hotel,
There's Maddie and Mosbey,
There's Zack and there's Cody
And London who loves me so well,
My owner is a rich hotel heiress,
I've been to New York, China and Paris,
I'm her dear little puppy and my name is not Lucky
I'm Evana who lives in a hotel.

Claudia Cousins (9)
Ightham Primary School, Sevenoaks

Long John Silver

We sailed along the Spanish waters,
A-searching for some gold,
We came across some merchantmen
And dropped them in the cold.

We sang a song of glory,
Upon the slimy deck,
But they were screaming sorely,
Whilst hanging by the neck.

The captain was a filthy man,
As dirty as his ship,
He would often use the ruthless whip,
Which hit you in the hip.

And on his leg a tattered boot,
With smothered, plastered mud,
Upon his face he had a scar,
It was as red as blood.

Millie Smith (8)
Ightham Primary School, Sevenoaks

Ten Endangered Whales

Ten endangered whales
Swimming in a line
'Harpoon them!' yelled the killers
Then there were nine

Nine endangered whales
Jumping very straight
'Dog meat!' cried the old man
Then there were eight

Eight endangered whales
Whistling up to Heaven
'Lipstick!' yelled the woman
Then there were seven

Seven endangered whales
Up to lots of tricks
'Tools!' boomed the workman
Then there were six

Six endangered whales
Down to the ocean bed they dive
'Fertilisers!' screamed the farmer
Then there were five

Five endangered whales
Lying dead on the ocean floor
Their whiskers to be used for bowstrings
Then there were four

Four endangered whales
Sinking
Down
Down
Down
Into the sea
Their bones to be used for corsets
Then there were three

Three endangered whales
Crying, 'We don't know what to do!'
Their blubber to be used for lamp oils
Then there were two

Two endangered whales
Wishing they could run
Their teeth to be used for craftwork
Then there was one

One endangered whale
All alone without its mum
'Kill! Kill! Kill!'
Cried the people
Then there were none

No endangered whales
Basking in the sun
Destroying endangered species in this world
Is this our idea of fun?

Louise Clelford (8)
Joy Lane Junior School, Sittingbourne

The Five-Eyed Horror Monster

Beware of the five-eyed horror monster,
That's lurking all around,
He'll be waiting somewhere to catch you,
When you're out and about.

He has five eyes
And only one leg,
He has a nose like a squashed mushroom
And teeth as sharp as knives.

He will be waiting in his lair,
For you to fall down the hole,
With his dinner plate rushing from side to side,
For you to fall upon.

He will cut you up
And chew you whole,
Bones, blood, flesh, all,
So keep clear of the five-eyed horror monster,
Or you will be next to go!

Emma Hance (11)
Lunsford Primary School, Aylesford

The Loony Thing

Loony has the body of a tarantula,
Eyes like a storm, flowing with fear,
A nose sharp and jagged like a great knife
And a mouth like a hidden cave.

Arms of a bull, short but strong,
Legs that have been there for years,
Wings green, mighty and besieging
Pincers that increase fear.

And friendly as a scorpion ready to strike,
With smaller scavengers scouring all over
And as clever as a goldfish with a brain,
As small as a crumb.

As loud as a dragon that is being tortured in a dungeon
And as smelly as a wet fox digging through the garbage
And as scary as a monster lurking around this poem,
With a target to strike . . . maybe it's you!

Jack Doyle (11)
Lunsford Primary School, Aylesford

Untitled

My monster has ears like lasers
And a hammer built in his arm,
The gun he picked up off the ground,
The horns off reindeer he found,
His teeth crush and grind.

One eye is bigger than the other,
He has an older brother,
His brother is taller and stronger,
He lurks in dungeons, deep,
But this one is more violent.

His ears are for turning things to dust,
You must not go near,
His dungeon is dark and dismal,
So never go near his palace,
Because it is dark and dismal down there.

Don't go too far from home, in case you're crushed,
You will know if he is in because of the smell,
His breath will put you to sleep,
If you go, don't try and peep,
You will be caught, by him, the monster.

He will crush you if you're alone,
His teeth will grind and tear,
His lasers will turn you to dust,
You must stay away, you must,
Or you will be crushed to dust,
You must not go down,
He will catch you, don't frown!

David Brooks (10)
Lunsford Primary School, Aylesford

The Minotaur

His eyes are as yellow as diamonds
And his legs are as muscular as lion's teeth.

His arms are overpowered like lion legs
And his tail endless like a ten-foot snake.

His body is gleaming like gold
And his legs are as powerful as a darting cheetah.

His tongue is for grabbing little children,
The spikes on his body are for keeping enemies away.

The cactus on his head is for
Pushing all his enemies out of the way, quick!

So stay out of the way of
The crashing, brainwashing monster,
The Minotaur.

Daniel Lee Banfield (11)
Lunsford Primary School, Aylesford

The Night Train

'Welcome to the night train,'
A weary voice we heard,
Here comes a bumpy ride,
The night train rides tonight,
Watch out tonight,
There might be a fright,
As the night train may go . . .
Boo!

A monster lurks beneath us,
He could jump out and eat us,
He's terrifying, crucifying,
But most of all - *ahhhh!*

It will demolish you,
Burn you,
He might even cook you.

Watch out he might be about,
With his ears as pointy as elves,
If you keep him waiting,
You could end up as . . .
Icing!

I'd run if I were you,
You'll end up as stew,
He'll grind you,
Wind you
And always find you!

Never ever go on this train,
Otherwise you'll end up as night train food!

Danielle Staples (11)
Lunsford Primary School, Aylesford

Scary Monsters Of Doom

My scary monster,
My monster has eyes like pools of blood,
His teeth are like sharp knives,
His ears are like elephant's ears,
His nose is like a pig's nose.

His body is like a tiger's body,
His claws are like a bear's claw,
His hair is like a hairy man's back,
His feet are like the size of a volcano.

If you go near my monster,
He will eat you like you were a piece of chicken,
If he eats you, your bones would only be left.

My monster smells like a bogeyman
And his breath smells like rubbish
And his feet smell like sick,
He runs like a ball.

My monster has a hammer,
The hammer is made out of metal
And the handle is made out of rock
And the spikes are made out of gold.

If you see my monster,
Do not go near it, or it might eat you,
Or hit you with his hammer!

Ryan Banfield (11)
Lunsford Primary School, Aylesford

The Monster From Under The Bed

From the cupboard,
To your bed,
Creeps the monster from under the bed.

His lava-red eyes help him see in the dark,
The antenna gives you terrifying nightmares,
His lumpy and hooked back,
Gives you such a bleak sleep.

His tortoiseshell-like tail whacks things,
Makes annoying sounds,
The greyness of its fur makes it
Invisible in the dark.

His shaggy coat helps it,
Be as quiet as a mouse.

So always check the cupboard first,
With an adult and not the bed,
Otherwise he'll eat you whole,
With his wolf-like head,
Beware of the monster from under the bed!

Joe Marks (11)
Lunsford Primary School, Aylesford

My Fluffy, Fuzzy Monster

As the sky turns bright,
This monster wakes to sunrise,
Steps out over the mist and comes into sight,
The fluffy, fuzzy monster.

Three eyes bunched, fur pink
Pupils like dark black beetles,
As cuddly as a puppy dog,
The fluffy, fuzzy monster.

He'll turn invisible when frightened,
He could ask you some day,
'Will you be my friend?'
the fluffy, fuzzy monster.

He loves making lots of friends,
He's as happy as a seal, spotting food,
As playful as a dolphin with a ball,
The fluffy, fuzzy monster.

He can be a bit mad,
He loves meeting different monsters,
But of course not ones bad,
The fluffy, fuzzy monster.

At the end of the day,
He'll return to his lair,
Lay in his bumpy bed and fall asleep,
My fluffy, fuzzy monster.

Angharad Morgan (10)
Lunsford Primary School, Aylesford

Spongey The Friendly Monster

My monster is called Spongey,
He's made out of sponge,
He wants to be scary,
But he's too much fun.

He loves sewing,
Every Saturday we go rowing,
He adores the beach
And sleeps in a sink.

He smells like a bonfire,
He has only one desire,
To have a full set of hair,
Then he will fly through the air.

Emily Farrell (11)
Lunsford Primary School, Aylesford

Bedtime

When you are fed,
He will be under your bed,
When you are asleep,
He will leap.

His arms can expand,
Like an elastic band,
His horns are as razor-sharp,
As a blade of a knife.

He has four eyes,
But they spy,
His scary eyes are as red as fire
And looks like criss-cross with wire.

He is spiky,
But he will kill you likely,
His teeth are sharp,
But his weakness is the sound of a harp.

If you play a lullaby quietly,
He will sleep quickly,
If you play it loudly,
He would act sleepy.

His tail would whip
You like a zip,
His body is as dark as the black sky
And quiet as a feather landing on the ground.

He does sound scary, but his name is Mary.

Adam Smith (10)
Lunsford Primary School, Aylesford

The Higmamegigamy Monster

When the day sleeps,
The higmamegigamy monster arises,
With a long drawn out sniff,
Of the perilous night air.

Then he silently stalks away,
With an untraceable step,
Transfixed on an unknown victim,
Who is unaware of her horrible fortune,
Which draws ever closer.

The house is in sight
And the door is locked,
But with a flick of his axe,
There comes a click,
His path is clear.

As he reaches the victim's room,
He swiped her teddy from her bed like taking candy from a baby,
He carefully puts his swag into his bag
And swiftly exits the room,
That poor, poor girl.

As he descends the stairs,
A soft 'ha' is issued,
From the monster's mouth,
With a triumphant air,
The higamemgigamy monster strides home.

The higamemgigamy monster
Morphs back into a boulder,
Waiting just waiting,
For the dark curtain to fall again
And his next . . . victim!

Jennifer Glover (11)
Lunsford Primary School, Aylesford

The Grark

The grark, he trails through the pitch-black streets,
The grark, only comes when he detects you're asleep,
Beware! His fearless fangs are like razors,
Keep away from his eyelash lasers.

The grark leaves a trail of thick green goo,
The grark, his brow is as big as an elephant,
You won't be able to leave his lair,
When he decides to take you there.

The grark came from planet Gloop,
The grark, he arrived in a bulging ball of sizzling fire,
If you get eaten by the grark,
Then one thing's for certain,
Afterwards everything goes dark!

The grark will come and see you soon,
The grark will bring his skeleton tack,
The skeleton tock is velvety red,
It will be all gory and red,
When it comes home with your head!

Gregg Harfleet (10)
Lunsford Primary School, Aylesford

Bounty Hunter

His scythe dripping wanted blood,
Screeching his sinister laugh,
Their pulse dead with a swish and a thud,
Leaving a trail of bloody . . . butchered . . . bodies sliced in half.

Tracking down monster's most wanted,
To earn their great bounty,
Making no friends for what he has done,
Travelling to creature's county.

He soars in with his drawn blade,
Fighting like a wolverine,
Never does he need aid,
Leaving a desolate and barren scene.

He leaves the place he has destroyed,
His black cloak shadows his face,
This is one monster you should avoid,
At any time or place.

George Hazelden (11)
Lunsford Primary School, Aylesford

Devious Devil

The monster came one day,
He came one day in May,
He arrived on the seventh
And departed on the eleventh,
Would you want to meet him?

He has bright red eyes
And sometimes flies,
His legs have crosses on the end
And his arms really extend,
Would you want to meet him?

He passed the tree
And the tree waved at me,
During the night,
The tree had such a fright,
Do you want to meet him?

He pounces on you like a cheetah,
Race him and he'll beat you,
When you're laying in your beautiful bed,
He will eagerly approach your head,
Do you want to meet him?

He left at night,
He went home late,
It was the end of the days,
Also the end of May,
Do you want to meet him?

Claire Martin (10)
Lunsford Primary School, Aylesford

Gull-A-Bull

Half bull,
Half bird,
Complete with ring,
I know, absurd!

Totally trickable,
He'll believe anything,
He has his own castle,
Of which he is king.

Where the trees linger,
Supporting the gloom,
Away from the woodcutters,
That spell their doom.

But be warned!
Don't reply - you never said,
If you get on his bad side,
He'll go charging off . . . to bed.

Jordan Summers (11)
Lunsford Primary School, Aylesford

Flying Fuzz

Flying Fuzz has eyes like dazzling diamonds,
His ears are like soft teddy bears,
But they're big, big, big!

His fur is a tiger's skin,
His claws are like needles,
But they're very sharp.

His eyes are as big as the glooming moon,
One on his head, and one on his forehead,
He can see you!

He flies as fast as the wind,
Searching the pitch-black sky for something,
Something special!
I wonder what?

Reece Wright (11)
Lunsford Primary School, Aylesford

The Demon

Beware the demon,
Who appears on Friday the 13th,
Who stalks in the night
And sleeps during the day,
Beware the demon . . . beware!

He will follow you until he catches you
And will grind you to a pulp,
He will set traps to capture you,
Then swallow your carcass! Gulp!
With blood dripping from his fangs.

Beware the massive Monster,
Whose scales are as hard as rock,
When he bursts into your room,
He will take whilst you are sleeping
And gives you a one way trip to his tomb.

In his deep, dark and dingy lair,
The worst goings on happen,
He impales you on spikes and cooks you alive
And dissolves your bones
And eats you for tea.

His blood-red skin
And poison-injected eyes,
Give this 8 foot 3 giant his evil,
With his skin-ripping claws,
He is impossible to miss.

You will know when he is coming,
Because the ground quivers and trembles,
He is as evil as the Devil
And that is why you should beware . . .
The Lesser Demon!

Connor Watson (10)
Lunsford Primary School, Aylesford

Jelly The Monster

My monster is made completely from jelly,
He slides around on his belly,
He's the kindest monster you've ever seen,
I can assure you that he's not mean!

Jelly the monster has sensors and arms,
Using these, he never harms,
In total he has eight eyes,
At the moment he's munching on jelly pies.

Some people say he's a freaky friend,
They like to drive him round the bend,
He's still as happy as the sun,
Because he's a lump of jelly fun.

Amber Aspinall (11)
Lunsford Primary School, Aylesford

I'm As Dizzy As My Name

I've got a head like a poisoned mushroom,
Arms with stars that are taken from the sky,
Eyes like a snake hypnotising its prey,
A body, as if the rainbow has been pinched from the sky,
I'm as dizzy as my name.

My slime is as glistening like a trail of fairy dust,
I have horns like fluorescent hands on my head,
Hands like a mutant humans,
The Devil's tail dyed blue and yellow,
I'm as dizzy as my name.

My neck is a blue giraffe's,
A nose bigger than my teachers,
Teeth that have become green,
With lips as dark as the swirling black hole,
I am dizzy the dizzer.

Katy Millgate (11)
Lunsford Primary School, Aylesford

My Monster Evlarg The Unbeatable

My monster has eyes like great balls of roaring flame,
My monster has a mouth like a brain-munching vampire,
My monster has legs like a bull's fur coat
And arms as spiky as a cactus,
A body as ugly as an ogre
And feet as big as a jumbo jet.

My monster is as friendly as . . .
A raging elephant's roar,
Has an appetite of a slimy sloth
And acts like a tyrannosaurus rex.

My monster will . . .
Squash your guts to a pimple,
Attack like there's no end
And eat you alive,

And that will be the end of your lives,
My monster Evlarg the Unbeatable.

Kieron Lee (11)
Lunsford Primary School, Aylesford

My Monster Fluffytree

Fluffytree has a furry coat, as pink as a flamingo
And even though she's brainless she likes to play bingo,
She has stars as antennae and hands,
But when she jumps, on all-fours she lands.

When she walks, she drags her floppy feet
And as she does this, she greets the people that she meets,
With her volcanic voice booming
And all the flowers blooming.

Her luminous green eyes,
Brighten up all the skies,
Her substantial, smiley songs,
Help make fantastic food served with tongs,
Fluffytree likes to go to the wood,
With her, she likes to take a pink picnic that tastes good,
Her bright, bulging, blue nose,
Gleams as light as her pongy toes.

Hannah Friel (11)
Lunsford Primary School, Aylesford

Monster Began

The way it walks,
It walks like a rhino,
Ready to fight its prey.

The way is speaks,
It speaks like a bird,
Singing in the morning.

The way it eats,
It eats like a pig,
Eating out of a trough.

The way it smells,
It smells like a sewer,
Ready to be emptied.

The way its claws are,
Claws are dragon's teeth,
Ready to fight.

The way its feet are,
Feet are like an elephant,
Stomping in the lake.

The way its breath smells,
Breath smells like a human,
Just finished eating a crab.

Leanne Ring (11)
Lunsford Primary School, Aylesford

Dordado Strikes

Dordado, Dordado is a mighty beast,
On children and pets he loves to feast,
If Dordado should give you a smile,
Don't be fooled, just run a mile.

He is wicked and nasty, vicious and cruel,
If you dare to go near him, you're a fool,
He lives in a big old cave,
But if you go in there you are brave.

He has poisonous scales on his back,
His spiky legs are brown and black,
Dordado, Dordado is a terrible sight,
Just a glimpse will fill you with fright.

Amy Hadley (11)
Lunsford Primary School, Aylesford

Bert The Honey Monster

A fat old monster by the name of Bert,
Said, 'Mummy, where's my shirt?'
Mummy said, 'It's here but,
You've been rolling in the dirt.

To teach you this you must not do,
Will make you wear a short tutu,'
'But Mummy,' said 'Bert, 'all the children will laugh,
Just like that cheeky giraffe.'

'Bert you are so big
And you have the manners of a pig,
Now, off to work you ugly ogre,
Or else I'll hit you with my poker.'

Poor little Bert, so sad and drowsy,
He didn't mean to be so lousy.

Shannon George (10)
Lunsford Primary School, Aylesford

Devil Bob

My monster has a body like a viper snake,
His face is like a fierce dragon,
He is as angry like a bear,
His legs are like jelly.

And he is not happy,
He's just like a vampire and not nice
But he likes people's blood,
He cuts them up like bones
And squashes them and eats them.

Luke Body (11)
Lunsford Primary School, Aylesford

The Hit Monster

Mr Blanc,
You'll see the flare,
You'll feel the hair,
But take guard, he's in the air.

His body is rough,
His skin is tough,
But take guard, he's in the air.

He's got polka dots on the face,
He's a disgrace,
But take guard, he's in the air.

He'll get you at night,
He'll put up a fight,
But take guard and watch out.

He'll kill without a sound,
He'll finish without a sound,
But take guard and watch out.

He'll take your blood,
He'll soak himself in a flood,
But take guard and watch out.

He'll be there at night,
He'll give you a fright,
But take guard he could be there.

He'll get you at night
And you're in for a fright.

Nicole Johnston (11)
Lunsford Primary School, Aylesford

Trendy!

There was once a friendly alien,
Her name was Trendy,
No matter who she met,
She would always be friendly.

She came down to Earth,
From a planet called Mars,
But she couldn't understand,
Why everyone drove cars.

She stopped a man,
He was as tall as a tree,
She was only three foot tall,
Only coming up to his knee.

She wanted to ask a question,
But she had to shout,
'Can you please tell me,
Why everyone rushes about?'

The man did not see her,
He walked straight past,
She gave a big sigh
And scurried off fast.

Trendy started to notice,
She was different in her looks,
Her eyes were crystals,
Instead of fingers, she had hooks.

She finally had enough
And decided to go back,
She started up her engine,
But the last thing that was heard,
Was a big loud
Crack!

Sophie Rideout (11)
Lunsford Primary School, Aylesford

Exfalador

Exfalador is a treacherous troll,
He lies in wait,
Ready to nibble at your soul,
Never forgetting to leave the bait,
Exfalador the treacherous troll.

Once inside its doomful ditch,
Its victims cry out in horror and disbelief,
As they spy Exfalador's wife the witch,
All because they fell through the trap, under a leaf.

Exfalador the treacherous troll,
One look at its algae-filled eyes,
Turns you quaking at the knees,
Its mutated skin folds over its thighs,
Its hair buzzes like a hive of bees,
Exfalador the treacherous troll.

Its feet are forests of untouched overgrown trees,
Its ears are fountains of golden earwax,
Exfalador's heart is set cold like stones in the breeze,
Its arms are in the shape of an axe,
Exfalador the treacherous troll.

Exfalador gobbles you up from head to toe,
It crunches your bones like a thresher thrashes corn,
It rips your body apart like your worst foe,
Its clothes are always tatty and torn,
Exfalador the treacherous troll.

At last we come to our final verse,
For poor old Exfalador was cursed,
Its wife the witch cursed it with a clever verse,
Now poor Exfalador will suffer the worst,
Exfalador the treacherous troll.

Rachel Jones (11)
Lunsford Primary School, Aylesford

What A Nice Dog

Being herded by the dog,
We were just running through the fog,
Didn't care what was at the end,
Running, running with the occasional bend,
Running through the nasty bog,
I trembled after stepping on a hedgehog,
The dog I thought was gonna gobble me up,
But the dog just came over and said,
'What's up?'
It turned out he wasn't so bad,
In fact I found out he was quite a nice lad.

Connor Fitzgerald (10)
Pembury Primary School, Tunbridge Wells

I Am An Eagle

I am an eagle, bird of prey,
I hunt not by night but I hunt through the day,
My razor-sharp talons pierce through tough skin,
My knife-like beak tears for meat that's within.

My wings are thin, they cut the air,
I glide with the wind from here to there,
I scan my land for something new,
Seeking it all, I fly askew.

When my day is at its end,
Through the thermals, I ascend,
To reach my cliff, my home, my nest,
It's then I lie, begin my rest.

Toby White (11)
Pembury Primary School, Tunbridge Wells

Dusky Dolphins

Acrobats of the sea,
Are dusty dolphins,
They swim in warm water,
They jump really high
And can dive really deep,
They are dusky dolphins.

Black and white is their skin,
Diving frequently,
Putting on a show,
They swim very far,
They are dusky dolphins.

Hannah Lancaster (10)
Pembury Primary School, Tunbridge Wells

Spring Days - Cinquain

Hooray!
The flowers bloom,
Birds start singing with joy,
A beautiful sweep of blue sky,
Hooray!

Kathryn Lawson-Wood (11)
Pembury Primary School, Tunbridge Wells

Clown

Smile maker,
Money taker.

Practised hard,
In his yard.

Good acrobat,
Silly hat.

No frown,
Just a silly clown.

Bethany Lambert (11)
Pembury Primary School, Tunbridge Wells

Kill The Dragon

Kill this dragon, kill him now,
Before he sends us all to Hell.

Slay him quick, slay him fast,
Send him back to his past.

He breathes his fire on my head,
Now I want him to be dead.

The little dragon looked quite sad,
Then I found he wasn't so bad.

We decided not to fight,
So he turned down his angry light.

We ended up being friends,
Which brought our fighting to an end.

Bethany Pike (11)
Pembury Primary School, Tunbridge Wells

Unwanted

I am a friendly breeding dog,
Though I'm treated like an unworthy hog,
They call me names, like 'Nasty Scrap,'
I'm whipped, I'm hit or even slapped.

Can't I ever see my puppies?
To see their grin and them so happy,
I never get some love,
Or a small hint from above.

No one cares,
No one shares,
No one listens,
Nothing glistens.

Oh my gosh, my legs aren't working,
My owners say that I am shirking

I bark and call and howl and yelp,
I'm always calling just for help,
All I want is a delicious feast,
Is that so hard for the angry beast?
I will never ever be fed,
For soon I think I will be dead.

Catherine Goldsmith (11)
Pembury Primary School, Tunbridge Wells

Summer's On My Mind

Hot summer evenings, playing out,
On my bike riding about,
Early sunsets, what lovely sights,
Full moons and long, light nights.

Summer is on my mind!

Flowers growing all around,
The little birds make no sound,
Early mornings, late nights,
On the beach, flying kites.

Summer is on my mind!

Summer's ended, I'm so sad,
But soon it's the weekend,
I'm so glad!

Lucy Gilchrist (10)
Sibertswold CE Primary School, Dover

Summer On My Mind

January is too cold,
All my clothes seem to fold.

I've got summer on my mind.

March is so boring,
It is always pouring,

April the sun rises slowly,
I don't want to get up early.

I've got summer on my mind.

Going camping when it's warm,
Early morning, always dawning,
Going to the beach,
Always trying to reach.

I've got summer on my mind.

It's better now,
I can go and play.

I've got summer on my mind.

Charlotte Powell (10)
Sibertswold CE Primary School, Dover

Summer On My Mind

Travelling to the seaside,
With all our buckets and spades,
Enjoying all the carousel rides,
Needing to wear your cool shades,
I have summer on my mind.

Barbecued sausages sizzling in the grate,
The lovely burnt smell of bacon,
Inviting round all our mates,
I have summer on my mind.

The luxurious taste of ice cream,
Picnicking round the pool,
Thinking of all your greatest dreams,
A soft breeze keeping me cool,
I have summer on my mind.

Emily Coupe (11)
Sibertswold CE Primary School, Dover

Summer On My Mind

Summer needs a cool breeze,
Although the pollen makes me sneeze,
Summer sun needs to cool down,
For that relaxing trip down the town,
Summer has light blue skies
And the evenings have stars on high,
Summer has long, late nights,
The boys all have their mud fights.

Summer, summer, summer,
Good old summer,
I have summer on my mind!

Summer is cool,
Go on and jump in the pool,
My dad looks like a fool,
Shorts and kagool,
No way!

'Finish your homework!'
I'm a tomboy, not a jerk,
I'm not going to finish my homework,
No way!

Summer, summer, summer,
Good old summer,
I've got summer on my mind!

Becky Brown (9)
Sibertswold CE Primary School, Dover

Summer On My Mind

January boring nights,
Jacob, playing with the kites,
Me, sitting listening to the gales,
Grandad, hitting hammer and nails,
When it's dry playing outside,
    I've got summer on my mind.

Riding horses,
Jacob setting courses,
I did well,
Mum fell,
    I've got summer on my mind.

Walking the dog,
Find a frog,
Nana cooking,
Mum looking,
Hot and sunny,
Toast and honey,
    I've got summer on my mind.

Luke Firth-Coppock (10)
Sibertswold CE Primary School, Dover

Summer On My Mind

Yeah! Summer, the fun starts now,
Running down the beach with a swimsuit and towel,
People having fun, splashing in the pool,
Charging about, trying to keep cool.

I've got summer on my mind.

Digging big holes with buckets and spades,
Ladies just sunbathing, wearing cool shades,
Having lots of barbecues,
The smoke gets in my eyes,
Staying up really late,
Watching green flies.

I've got summer on my mind.

Going to bed at about midnight,
Many mosquitoes, cor! Do they bite!
Can't wait till tomorrow, big water fight!

Annabel Reville (10)
Sibertswold CE Primary School, Dover

Summer On My Mind

Autumn is wet,
I bet,
Leaves are falling,
I hear Dad calling.

I've got summer on my mind.

Winter mornings are too cold,
My nan is getting far too old.

I've got summer on my mind.

Spring is here,
I fear.

I've got summer on my mind.

Playing down the beach,
Hearing babies screech,
Towel round me,
Watching a bee.

Summer's on my mind.

Shannah Hall (10)
Sibertswold CE Primary School, Dover

Summer On My Mind

The hot sun gleams,
When I watch cricket teams,
The smoky pong of barbecues
And the summer birds' merry crow . . .

I've got summer on my mind.

I wake up early,
With my hair all curly,
Go outside - walk my dog,
Amy with a burger - what a hog!

I've got summer on my mind.

The warm summer sun feels like a blanket,
Hot in Dad's old car - you've got to crank it!
Fishing by the cool river,
Did you know - fish oil is good for the liver . . .

I've got summer on my mind.

Tom Harman (10)
Sibertswold CE Primary School, Dover

Summer On My Mind

I like it when it's winter,
I like it when it's springtime,
I like it when it's autumn,
But most of all, I love it when it's summer,
I have summer on my mind.

I love it when I'm outside,
In all the warm fresh air,
Out there, it's my life!
Sitting in the old oak tree,
Slurping melting ice cream,
I have summer on my mind.

Building camps,
Is my favourite thing,
I have summer on my mind.

I prowl around under a canopy of leaves,
Hoping not to get stung by lots of bees,
Behind bushes, I feel like a king,
Singing to myself,
Summer's definitely on my mind.

I love it when it's morning,
When the grass is luscious and deluxe
And for a walk I take my dog Lucy Louie!

I have summer on my mind!

Claire Penny (9)
Sibertswold CE Primary School, Dover

Summer On My Mind

Wake up in the morning,
All sunny outside,
Get dressed and ready,
To start the day alive.

I step outside and
Summer's on my mind.

Run to the swings,
They're the best,
Run to the beach,
Take off my vest.

I step outside and
Summer's on my mind.

The evenings round the campfire,
Warm and fun they are,
Late nights are cosy,
Watching for a star.

I step outside and
Summer's on my mind.

Ruby Russell (10)
Sibertswold CE Primary School, Dover

Summer On My Mind

I am at the beach,
Rock pool glistening
And I am listening,
To the noisy crowds.

I've got summer on my mind.

People call me,
For my tea,
Don't wanna go,
So I'll be slow.

I've got summer on my mind.

I'm sunbathing now,
Turning different shades,
I'm going to play,
With buckets and spades.

I've got summer on my mind.

Abigail McLean (10)
Sibertswold CE Primary School, Dover

Summer's On My Mind

Lazy evenings, watching TV,
Summer's on my mind.

Out on my bike,
Until late at night,
Summer's on my mind.

Water fights in the garden with friends,
Summer's on my mind.

Lunch under the yellow, hot sun,
Summer's on my mind.

Eating sandwiches with pals,
Summer's on my mind.

Going to the seaside, getting ice cream,
Summer's on my mind.

Summer's going to be great!

Laura Palmer (10)
Sibertswold CE Primary School, Dover

A Rainbow

Red is like a rose,
Blue is like the blue, bright sky,
Green is like the grass, swaying through the breeze,
Orange is like the fiery lava in a volcano,
Yellow is like a lovely bright centre of a daisy,
Violet is a calm, soothing colour,
Purple is a dark colour in a sunset.

Daniel Westbrook (9)
Sibertswold CE Primary School, Dover

Sweets

The colour of sweets are bright and lively,
It makes you get up and play.

The taste of sweets is sweet and sour.

Sweets look like little funny things,
Which I want to gobble up.

Chocolate is just like honey,
I want to gobble it up
And put it in my tummy.

Sweets remind me of something sour,
Sizzling in my mouth.

Gobstoppers can break your teeth
But really they are sweet and sour.

Amy Hill (9)
Sibertswold CE Primary School, Dover

Can We Go To The Zoo?

Can we go to the zoo?
Because I'd rather go to the zoo than stay at home with you.

There's monkeys and hares,
Tigers and bears.

All the monkeys swinging to and fro,
'Oh please Mum, can't we go?

Oh yeah, and there's ice cream,
Come on let's go or I'll scream!

Can we go on a rowing boat,
Go and grab your coat.

Oh Mum, just for a quick visit . . .
Mum, what is it?'

Zzzzzzz . . .

Oh great she's gone to sleep,
Now I'll just have to stay at home and weep.

Hannah Coupe (9)
Sibertswold CE Primary School, Dover

Love

The colour of love is a calm and comforting pink,
Love sounds like a warm and peaceful song,
Love tastes like milky warm hot chocolate,
Love smells like a beautiful perfume being sprayed,
Love looks like two bunnies, sitting next to each other,
Love feels like a soft cat's fur,
Love reminds me of my mum and dad's wedding photo.

Laura Winter (9)
Sibertswold CE Primary School, Dover

Happiness

Happiness is bright yellow and orange,
Happiness sounds like children playing
And happiness sounds like people at the beach having fun,
Happiness tastes like chocolate ice cream and warm curries,
It smells like roses and honey,
It looks like a big yellow sun,
It feels like a warm breeze,
It reminds me of my holiday that I enjoyed!

Sarah Penny (10)
Sibertswold CE Primary School, Dover

Darkness

In the dark where no one goes,
Lives a big powerful monster down below,
In a dingy, scary, fearsome cave
And in the middle of the night the beast awakes,
Because when the full moon is up,
He goes out looking for flesh and blood.

Thomas Duncan (8)
Sibertswold CE Primary School, Dover

The Ultimate Poem

In World War I, we soldiers will die,
As we march forth towards the enemy's front line,
Guns ablazing, we get shot,
The men in their trenches still praying, praying that
                         they will survive,
You can hear the wounded crying out for help,
All poppies brushing along our legs,
All we care about is protecting our country,
At first I thought it was a good idea,
But as it went on, it seemed more and more frightening,
We will all die in Flanders fields.

Charles Harman (9)
Sibertswold CE Primary School, Dover

Hate

Hate is the colour of yellow,
Hate sounds like someone's older sister punching her little brother,
Hate tastes like a bitter lemon being eaten,
Hate smells like poison that's just been laid,
Hate looks like people fighting fiercely round
A volcano that has just erupted,
Hate feels like seeing someone you love die,
It reminds me of me and my sister fighting.

Jonathan Allen (9)
Sibertswold CE Primary School, Dover

Anger

Anger is red like a fierce lion,
Anger sounds like a loud, low noise,
Anger tastes like three hot chillies in your mouth,
Anger smells like a train with too much coal in it,
Anger looks red like a red woolly jumper,
Anger feels like you have just been tormented for two hours,
Anger reminds me of a big, red, scary monster.

Wil Green (9)
Sibertswold CE Primary School, Dover

Anger

Anger is like the sun, burning bright,
It's red like tomato ketchup.
Anger sounds like a fire blazing in the night.
Anger tastes like acrid smoke choking someone.
Anger smells like danger ahead.
Anger looks like thunder breaking through the clouds.
Anger reminds me of death.

Jordan Witts (9)
Sibertswold CE Primary School, Dover

Sadness!

The colour of sadness is blue, bright blue,
Sadness sounds like a blizzard, rushing through
                              the trees and bushes,
Sadness tastes like a tear running down your cheek
And into your mouth,
Sadness smells of a freezing, cold night when
You're outside,
Sadness looks like you're putting your head into a freezer
And you cry of sadness,
Sadness feels like you're putting your head under
A freezing cold hose and it's dripping down your back,
Sadness reminds me of a roaring sea blowing everywhere.

Daisy Hobbs (9)
Sibertswold CE Primary School, Dover

Death

Death is full of darkness and it is black,
Death sounds like people screaming for help,
Death tastes like burnt food,
Death smells damp and wet,
Death looks like total darkness,
Death feels cold and icy,
Death reminds me of people screeching.

Jacob Roberts (9)
Sibertswold CE Primary School, Dover

Love

The colour of love is purple,
The sound of love is like birds singing,
The taste of love is like sweet sugar,
The smell of love is like lavender,
The thing that love looks like is a baby being born,
The thing that love feels like is you're fast asleep,
The thing that love reminds me of is
My nice comfy bed.

Alexander Byrne (9)
Sibertswold CE Primary School, Dover

Hate

Hate is like the colour black disliking your best mate,
Hate is like the sound of killing screams when you are mad,
Hate is like the crunchy bones breaking in your body,
Hate is like the smell of acrid smoke choking you,
Hate is like the angry look on a bull about to charge,
Hate feels like the hardest brick hitting you in the head,
Hate reminds me of a person in the street yelling at me.

Harry Miller (9)
Sibertswold CE Primary School, Dover

Summer, Winter, Spring, Fun

S un is red,
U nbored,
M y ice cream is melting,
M e on the beach,
E veryone happy,
R ight, everyone jump in the sea, 1 . . . 2 . . . 3 . . . jump!

W hy?
I n the snow,
N ever going to get out,
T ogether,
E veryone is happy,
R ight let's go in . . . *brrr*.

S pring,
P ride,
R hymes,
I nside, no!
N ever,
G iving up!

F unny,
U pset (not!)
N ever sad.

Jessica Doble (10)
Sibertswold CE Primary School, Dover

My Shopping Trip

I went to Canterbury to get some stuff,
Because if I stayed at home,
My brother will get in a huff,
I went to *Tammy* and *New Look*,
Clothes went out and my money was taken.

I don't have much money now,
I saw some shoes called *How,*
I wanted them but I don't want to be a cow
And that was my shopping trip
And it's ended now.

Laura Castledine (9)
Sibertswold CE Primary School, Dover

Sour

Sour is the colour of bright green,
Sour tastes like little bitter things being mean,
Sour sounds like screeching noises,
Sour looks like greeny bubbles,
Sour smells like boiling trouble,
Sour feels like it's sizzling in your mouth,
Sour reminds me of sweets!

Hannah Butcher (9)
Sibertswold CE Primary School, Dover

Love

Love is the colour of soft red,
Love sounds like soft music playing in the background,
It tastes like a sweet,
Love smells like a lovely perfume,
Love looks like lots of doves flying,
It makes you feel happy and joyful,
It reminds me of a wedding taking place,
Two cats in love.

Courtney Forrest (8)
Sibertswold CE Primary School, Dover

Hungry

Hungry, I saw this burger,
Gorgeous and scrumptious,
I could feel the ketchup flowing down my throat,
I couldn't stop looking,
The feel in my throat,
I was having a dream about owning a burger bar,
I couldn't stop thinking, I pounced
But I smacked into the window,
I suddenly imagined lying in burgers.

Stuart Lindsay (9)
Sibertswold CE Primary School, Dover

Fear

Fear is the colour purple,
Fear sounds like a ghost in a haunted castle,
Fear tastes like something like garlic which you hate,
Fear smells like something you hate and fear,
Fear looks like a horrible sight coming towards you,
Fear feels like a ghost touching you but you can't feel it,
Fear reminds me of heights.

Jack Miller (8)
Sibertswold CE Primary School, Dover

The Great Night Rider

In the darkness of the night,
Night rider was out, I don't know where he was going,
He was on one of his most beautiful horses,
I followed him, he was going to the West Indies.

Five hours later when he got there,
He and horse were tired from the long journey,
He stayed in the West Indies for a day,
Then in the night he set off again,
Delivering mail to the people of California,
Then the night rider came back,
Happy and cheerful.

Remy Beasley (9)
Sibertswold CE Primary School, Dover

The Creature

The creature is mighty,
The creature is bright,
Come to my house and let's have a fight.

It lives in a dark, gloomy cave,
That no one has ever seen,
But one weird lady said 'I have been,'
'Sure you have - in your dreams.'

'I'll show you lot,'
'You better not be lying.'

So one old foggy day,
During the month of May,
Here was one deep cave,
Inside one enormous rocky mountain.

When it came out with a mighty roar,
It looked like my teacher from Year 4.

'Sorry my lady you are so right,'
I didn't know you were so bright.'

'I'm so glad it was so true because it was in my son's
Midnight dreams!'
Then the lady suddenly vanished in a green beam!

'Oh my goodness where did she go?'
I wonder if she will meet my friend Mo?
Who also vanished in a green beam.

I wonder if she's with aliens now!

Connor Stickings (11)
St Augustine of Canterbury Catholic Primary School, Gillingham

The Green-Eyed Monster

Deep in the mud pit the great monster creeps,
Snore, snore, the great monster sleeps.

Creakety, creak, along the floorboards,
The bang, clang, flanging of doors.

Shhh, shhh, the tap slowly drips,
Slurp, slurp the great monster sips.

Under the duvet the great monster leaps,
Wahh, wahh, the great monster weeps.

'It's not fair!' the great monster cries,
'That chocolate cake was my surprise.'

The green-eyed monster, so angry,
Had a swim in the jealous sea.

Georgie Brace (11)
St Augustine of Canterbury Catholic Primary School, Gillingham

The Hunt

His habitat gets noisier every day,
There he shall wait till he sights his prey,
His eyes flitting wildly like a hawk,
Around the playground he begins to stalk.

Nervously hiding in the lunch hall,
Eating silently, alone by a wall,
Time is up! The prey must go,
Out to the playground he faces his foe.

Casually the predator walks out,
The pack looks on, then spread about,
The boy is seen, he has to run!
He falls, surely the bullies have won?

Up he jumps, the bullies close in,
He feels claws on his back, tearing,
The prey is caught, the predator shouts,
'Tell no one of this, you little lout.'

'We'll get you, Weedy, after school,'
They push him up against the wall,
He then realises he must tell,
Since he is in a bullying hell.

The teacher listens with careful ears,
Then leaves the boy, still in tears,
She marches out of the school gate,
To where the bullies lie in wait.

The leader's caught the troop desert,
Now it's predator who begins to hurt,
The bully is punished, all is well,
Remember if you're bullied, just *tell!*

Don't suffer in silence, tell someone!

Katherine Parry (11)
St Augustine of Canterbury Catholic Primary School, Gillingham

Wildlife Poem

W hales splash out water in the air,
I nsects crawl everywhere,
L ittle beasts find it no warmer,
D anger is round the corner,
L eaves sway side to side,
I f I were you, I'd quickly hide,
F ear no more,
E ager though lions want to roar!

Megan Gough (10)
St Augustine of Canterbury Catholic Primary School, Gillingham

The Jungle

T errific animals come out to play,
H yenas laughing all day,
E lephants squirt water all day.

J umping cheetahs and leopards race,
U nder the trees are swinging monkeys,
N oises appear all around me,
G iraffes peer round from the bushes,
L ions roar with their manes blowing,
E very night the noises stop, stop, stop.

Lauren Catherine Chamberlain (10)
St Augustine of Canterbury Catholic Primary School, Gillingham

Mouse Kennings

Cheese eater
Small squeaker
Cat's dinner
Cheesy grinner
Fast mover
Wire chewer
Elephant scarer
Fur wearer
Floor scrambler
Scrap hunter.

Daniel Johnston (11)
St Augustine of Canterbury Catholic Primary School, Gillingham

The Simpsons

S tupid
I immature
M oaning
P reposterous
S illy
O n the couch
N ever
S ensible

H ungry
O verweight
M onster
E nvies
R ich people

M um
A verage
R efreshes
G rumpy
E lderly

B urping
A nnoying
R ated
T oo much of a prankster

L oving
I maginative
S ensible
A bsolutely loves learning
   and the little baby Maggie too.

Sam James Crockford (10)
St Augustine of Canterbury Catholic Primary School, Gillingham

World Cup

W e rule the pitch, we rule the ball,
O ver the goalie into the goal,
R ound the defenders, into the goal,
L oudly the crowd roar and roar
D ribbling the ball around the pitch

C ome on England!
U nder the post and into the goal,
P ower is needed if you want to succeed.

Samuel Richardson (9)
St Augustine of Canterbury Catholic Primary School, Gillingham

The Wicked World Of Brazil

Brazil will fight all through the night
And brighten up the pitch with their yellow shirts.
They will bury the ball in the back of the net
And Ronaldo will shoot,
It will go through the netting,
Brazil are my heroes.

Jacob Hart-Lane (10)
St Augustine of Canterbury Catholic Primary School, Gillingham

My Favourite Cousin David

You're the bright red rose that glows in the
Queen's garden in the moonlight.

The twinkle in your eyes glows as you blink.

You're as elegant as a piano's notes and as mucky as mud.

You're the glistening sun that lights up my day,
Without you there wouldn't be light.

Your laugh is as wild as a hyena and as funny as a comedian.

The fun we have is never to forget!
You are my favourite cousin,
This I will *never regret!*

Emily Louisa Fallon (9)
St Augustine of Canterbury Catholic Primary School, Gillingham

Cats

C ats are very cute,
A ll night they sleep, all night!
T each your cat to do tricks,
S ooty is my cat and gets on my nerves!

Alice Sivyer (10)
St Augustine of Canterbury Catholic Primary School, Gillingham

Untitled

P eaches is a very fluffy cat,
E ating away on a tray,
A lot of food is not her best choice,
C arrots and cucumber is one of her choices,
H er friend is Peter, he is a meat eater,
E ating the meat off the plate,
S o the story ends with two old cats, who eat a lot of batter.

Shane Cox (10)
St Augustine of Canterbury Catholic Primary School, Gillingham

My Garden In Spring

This is my garden when spring has begun,
Outside we have fun, under the golden sun,
There are lots of vibrant colours and colourful flowers,
There are bees, butterflies, wasps and worms
And lots of other things that squirm,
Birds like sparrows, blue tits too,
There are tall trees with pure green leaves,
Lush green grass grows up tall,
Compared to my garden, I feel very small.

Hannah Wadey (8)
St Michael's CE Junior School, Maidstone

Mon Ami Pierrot

Mon Ami Pierrot,
How to describe him,
He always speaks French,
Yet he comes from London.

As my family and I,
Skip to the park,
He wanders the fields
And calls out d'leau.

When we go to church,
He swims in the sea,
They say he'll drown,
But that doesn't bother me.

We watch him, amazed,
As he swims like a dolphin,
But when we call for him,
He vanished into blackness.

One day he did not come,
For a very long time,
A salt death he had,
But at least he died at sea,
With the dolphins and whales,
In his greatest dreams.

Laura Sage (11)
St Peter's Catholic Primary School, Sittingbourne

Snake And Croc - Haikus

Snake

Scaly bumpy skin,
With huge amounts of venom,
The pit viper strikes.

Croc

Hard, rough, bumpy skin,
Strikes out of murky water,
The saltwater croc.

Anthony Burbury (10)
St Peter's Catholic Primary School, Sittingbourne

The Scary Dragon

T he grey, dull, scary dragon living on a mountain far,
H eat from mouth, lighting the night sky,
E ating every human in its path.

S cary dragon with bloody teeth,
C reep close to a weapon, dragon is near,
A fire breather deadly to all,
R ight it's time for the king to send a knight,
Y ou are the people running from such a fright.

D ragon creeping nearer getting scarier,
R ight now we should be moving
A nd now I can hear the screaming,
G onna run but can't, too scared and frozen,
O n this day, I meet the creature,
N ow it's my turn to tackle this monster's pain.

Matthew Jones (11)
St Peter's Catholic Primary School, Sittingbourne

Crocodile

If you've ever wondered what crocodile means, here it is:

C is for cunning, as cunning as a fox,
R is for robust, as robust as a mountain,
O is for obstacle, just an obstacle in the water,
C is for concerning, concerning all the locals,
O is for obsessed, making the locals obsessed,
D is for disguise, able to disguise in murky water,
I is for illuminate, when lights shine, eyes illuminate,
L is for lightning fast, as fast as a torpedo,
E is for eroding, slowly eroding away.

Matthew Burbury (10)
St Peter's Catholic Primary School, Sittingbourne

England FC

E ngland will win the World Cup!
N ever again will they lose a match,
G ood isn't what they are, they're excellent,
L oving every minute of the game,
A mazing skills and young players,
N o one can beat them,
D eadly shots flying past the keeper.

F ootball players in world-class kits,
C heating players not in our squad.

Lachlan Hutton (11)
St Peter's Catholic Primary School, Sittingbourne

Teeth

Glowing in the night,
Breath smelling of fresh Murray Mints,
Smiling without fear.

Tom Farren (11)
St Peter's Catholic Primary School, Sittingbourne

Touring Cars

As slidey as oil,
As fast as a rocket,
As slick as tyres,
Very noisy exhausts,
As booming as a monster truck.

Ben Avery (10)
St Peter's Catholic Primary School, Sittingbourne

Brand New

It's like a new toy,
With a button nose and strong arms and legs . . .
But it's not,
So small, smaller than me,
Hiding in darkness, where it cannot be seen.

What is it?
I can't see,
There it was, it sounds like a toy,
But it's not,
I see a leg and an arm,
It's a baby girl . . . I was wrong.

Nicola Rodgers (10)
St Peter's Catholic Primary School, Sittingbourne

Mike

Mike loves riding on his bike,
To go fishing he walks a hike,
The biggest fish he's caught is a pike,
Good old Mike.

Mike loves the sports brand *Nike*,
He rides to the shop on his bike,
If he falls off he shouts out, *'Yikes!'*
Good old Mike.

David Robertson (10)
St Peter's Catholic Primary School, Sittingbourne

Jamal And David

Jamal and David run like the wind,
Asafa Powell has the speed of lightning,
We should run for England that is true,
Even though we're young and new,
Jamal has fast legs and David is strong,
The Olympics is where we belong.

David Williams (10)
St Peter's Catholic Primary School, Sittingbourne

Summer

Summer's like hot fires,
Spreading round England like hot tyres,
Going to the water on the beach,
Having an ice cream to cool you down,
From the sun beams,
Summer's the best.

Abimbola Ogunyemi (9)
St Peter's Catholic Primary School, Sittingbourne

My Best Friend

Animal lover,
Ear bender,
Disco diva,
Loyal friend,
Always there,
A shoulder to cry on,
A good laugh,
Never a frown upon her face,
Funny,
Caring,
Loving,
Kind,
That's my best friend!

Poppi-Anna Conway (10)
St Peter's Catholic Primary School, Sittingbourne

There's Someone In My Head

There's someone in my mind,
He's in there all the time,
I play games with him but I always win.

He puts me to my rest, when I have a test,
He may be annoying but how I love him!

Ellie Haddock (9)
St Peter's Catholic Primary School, Sittingbourne

My Dad Kennings

Football mad,
Yabber yabber,
Funny bunny,
Kick it up,
Careful eater,
Great cooker,
Mad hatter,
Bit stressed,
Not a fool,
That is why he's so cool!
My dad.

Grace Butcher (10)
St Peter's Catholic Primary School, Sittingbourne

My Dad

A daughter lover,
An Ireland supporter,
A rugby follower,
A dinner cooker,
A brilliant chef,
A cheerer-upper,
A tummy tickler,
A big hugger,
A spider catcher,
A funny man, my dad.

Poppy Byrne (10)
St Peter's Catholic Primary School, Sittingbourne

In My Head

In my head is a bubbling brain,
In my head is a calculating computer,
In my head is a loyal friend,
In my head is an overflowing drink of knowledge!
In my head is me!
Just plain me!

Lauren Etherington (10)
St Peter's Catholic Primary School, Sittingbourne

Kennings Cat

Dog runner,
Mouse chaser,
String player,
Fish eater,
Purring sleeper,
Tree climber,
Running rocket,
Nine life jumper,
Flea scratcher,
Bird killing machine.

Christopher Harimat (9)
St Peter's Catholic Primary School, Sittingbourne

My Sister

My sister is a gurgle machine,
She's small and cute.

My sister is cheerful,
She looks like me.

My sister is pretty,
She likes kitties.

My sister is special to me,
She makes me fill up with glee.

My sister is so cool,
She is not a total fool.

Heather Barton (10)
St Peter's Catholic Primary School, Sittingbourne

My Flea Catcher

I had a flea catcher,
Also an ear scratcher,
Playful snatcher.

A fast runner,
Likes the summer.

He's called Plug,
He likes to snuggle up.

Zoe Thomas (10)
St Peter's Catholic Primary School, Sittingbourne

My Friend

My friend is funny,
She is cool,
She never ever looks like a fool,
She's a vegetarian,
A librarian,
She's a clown and she never frowns.

Layla-Autumn Harris (10)
St Peter's Catholic Primary School, Sittingbourne

My Sister

My sister is called Larrissa,
She is always in the way,
We argue every day,
But I still love her in every way,
She loves me in June, October, November and May,
She teases me,
I sometimes feel I need to be free,
But maybe . . .
Well we'll see.

Brieanna Way (10)
St Peter's Catholic Primary School, Sittingbourne

Football Kit

F antastically beautiful red, white and blue,
O bviously great colours,
O ut of this world,
T ogether it creates Oak's kit,
B y the way 20 is my number,
A t the moment I'm top scorer,
L et me tell you I'm a striker,
L ike I said I'm a striker.

K icking the ball into the goal,
I have scored 32 goals,
T om Sewell is my name.

Tom Sewell (10)
St Peter's Catholic Primary School, Sittingbourne

My Mum

My mum is the best person in the world,
She is my best friend, my mate.
She cares for me,
My mum is great!

My mum helps me when I am doing my homework,
When there is a hard sum.
She loves me very much
And I love Mum!

Eleanor Page (10)
St Peter's Catholic Primary School, Sittingbourne

My Best Friend

She turns a frown upside down,
Makes you feel like you have a crown,
Gives a smile when skies are grey,
Makes you angry? No way!
She's the top, she makes you pop!
She makes me mad! She makes me glad!
She's everything you want her to be,
Sorry, you can't have her, she's with me,
Because she's my best friend!

Deborah Shangobiyi (10)
St Peter's Catholic Primary School, Sittingbourne

On The Farm

Lambs white as snow,
Soft as wool,
Skipping in the long fresh grass,
Bleating for their mums.

Tractors brand new,
With the plough behind,
Like massive green ships,
Sailing through the sea,
Leaving waves behind.

Farmers in dirty overalls,
Trudging through the fields,
To feed the sheep.

Planting strawberries,
With poly-tunnels on top,
I think of juicy ruby-red fruit,
With sugar and cream!

Joe Chapman (10)
West Malling Primary School, West Malling

Simile Girl

Hair as thick as a tree trunk,
Eyes as black as coal,
Nose as pointed as a piece of glass,
Body as fat as an elephant,
Mouth as wide as a football,
Hands as big as my dad's feet,
Legs as long as a table,
Feet as big as umbrellas.

Megan Locke (10)
West Malling Primary School, West Malling

The Spider Is Scared . . .

I'm a web spinner,
I'm a slow stalker,
I'm a little scarer,
Fly eater,
Bird watcher
And a very fast killer.

Harry Stansfield (10)
West Malling Primary School, West Malling

The Dolphin Song

Neither fingers nor thumbs have I,
But I glide through the water
And I can,
Swim, swim, swim.

Neither legs nor arms have I,
But I have fins to jump
And I can,
Swim, swim, swim.

I master every movement,
For I eat, swim and jump
And I can,
Swim, swim, swim.

Amy Thompson (11)
West Malling Primary School, West Malling

Teachers

Teachers, teachers, they're such a nag,
All they need around their mouth is a little gag,
Please, please help us,
The least you can do is drive them away in a bus.

Zoey Nettleingham (10)
West Malling Primary School, West Malling

Rosie The Cat

Night hunter
Tree climber
Mouse chaser
Bed taker
Bird killer.

Rosie the cat.

Tom Steer (11)
West Malling Primary School, West Malling

The Chocolate Song

I love chocolate,
Chocolate is my Heaven,
You have one and I will have seven,
Don't take my chocolate,
It's mine, mine all mine,
You will be fine.

I love chocolate,
It's my number one thing,
My nan says I'll go ping,
But I don't care,
I might share,
I love, love, love my chocolate.

I love chocolate,
Chocolate is the best,
It beats the rest,
I think I want a chocolate fountain,
Or a chocolate mountain!

Chloe Cooke (11)
West Malling Primary School, West Malling